A Tar Pit to Dye In

A Tar Pit to Dye In

Poems by

Ed Werstein

Kelsay Books

ISBN: 978-1-947465-45-9

Kelsay Books
Aldrich Press
www.kelsaybooks.com

For Sylvia, my first and best reader

Acknowledgments

I would like to thank the following journals and anthologies for first publishing some of the poems in this book:

Poemeleon: "At Home and Barefoot"
Soundings: "Newport Poetry Trail"
Peninsula Poets: "The Best We Can Hope For," "Citizen of the World," "Habits," "In Walked So and So," and "Sage Advice"
Poetry Dispatch: "The White Bicycle"
Wisconsin Poets Calendar: "Afterlife," "Licorice Lollipops," "Supply and Demand," and "Red-winged Sentry"
Verse-Virtual: "You Could Google It," "Spineless Thief," "Actually," "Poetic Language," and "The Moon is Always Female," and "Her Tea Bag Waits"
Red Cedar Review: "Dear Internet," "Organ Grinder," and "Questions for Mati"
Stoneboat: "Caution!," "Anthony's Hands," "Experiment in Valdivia, "The Geography of Penelope Cruz," "Eskimo Medicine," "First World Problem," and "Meditation on My Sandwich"
Vampyr Verse: "Nosferatu's Garden"
Twice Told Tales: "Fairy Tale Tabloid"
Gyroscope Review: "Helium," "Grand Unified Theory," "Nick Chopper," and "The Prophet as Chemist"
Grit, Gravity, and Grace: "The Attack of the Pneumonia Gang"
Switched-on Gutenberg: "Handball Elder"
Screech Owl: "Save This Poem"
Your Daily Poem: "Sleep"
The Camel Saloon: "Still Life," "Venus of Delta," "Fuse," "Memo on a Parable," and "Fences"
Echoes: "Perspectives,"and "Revision"
Steam Ticket: "Kooser's Groupies"
Tawdry Bawdry: "The Picture of Dorian Redwood"

Hummingbird: "Apolitically"

Verse Wisconsin: "We All Lay Down," and "Your Cue"

Blue Collar Review: "Gardening in Babylon," "Droning On,"
"Campaign Promises," "Mine," and "Teaching Women How to Fly"

New Verse News: "Fog Forces the Cancellation," "Playing Cards,"
"Another Useless Headline Poem," "Lint," and "Austerity"

Bramble: "Love Trumps Hate"

Burdock: "Lorca For Beginners"

"Watching Gulls Fish on the Fox", "Accidental Poem," "I'm Not Where I Belong," and "Apostrophe S" first appeared in the book *Masquerades and Misdemeanors,* the poetry of the Hartford Avenue Poets (Pebblebrook Press, 2013).

Contents

III. Taking the Needle

I. A Footrunner from Thebes

It's just a poem
it's seventeen syllables
but it's not haiku

At Home and Barefoot

Like a discalced Carmelite
I'm barefoot again.
Poetry's the culprit, always poetry.

I don't know why the reaction
manifests (pedifests?) itself in my feet,
but it is less painful than having
the top of my head taken off.

This morning it was a line from di Prima,
the only war that matters is the war against the imagination
I halted
re-read the line
and felt the chill.

I looked down on my exposed toes
and my Goldtoes lying there
halfway to the wall.

It might be Stafford,
Your one little fire that will start again
or Ferlinghetti comparing Willie Mays
to a footrunner from Thebes.

The first time it happened
it was a line from Levertov,
Tolerance, what crimes are committed in your name
and I felt the air between my toes
my socks launched with such force
they were airborne.

I don't have the same problem
in the library or the park
or on the bus, but tell me,
who reads poetry at home
with their shoes on?

The Best We Can Hope For

No clear boundary
separates happiness from unhappiness
no border to cross
from one state into the other.

We stand on sand
shifting
straddling both feelings at once.

Elation and despair
are opposites
on either side of some equilibrium
we cannot define.
No horizon, no line
separates tower from well.

An hourglass floating
horizontal
on an undulating sea
tilting sometimes toward
sometimes away
is the best we can hope for.

If the glass ever righted itself
happiness would flow out
emptying into despair
which is the same
as our time running out.

Watching Gulls Fish on the Fox

I wish I could float down the stream
of ideas flowing through my mind
and bring up poem after poem
the way the gulls floating here
bring up fish after fish.

Perhaps this is just a rich
stretch of river to fish.
More likely it is the way
the late afternoon sun catches their scales
right here where the Fox flows east
before turning north again.

The birds float backward
facing west, heads bent,
bobbing down and bringing them up
one after the other,
then abruptly fly back upstream,
ready for another ride,
the way a child jumps off a merry-go-round
and runs right back in line.

I wish I could find a spot like this
on my mind's river.
I'd float there all day bobbing
bringing up poem after poem
and putting them down.

And every once in a while,
I'd bring up one too big
to get down all at once.
Every once in a while,

I'd bring up one gleaming in the sunlight,
flopping out of both sides of my notebook,
and be forced to fly to the nearest bank
and set it down and work on it awhile.

Newport Poetry Trail

At the Lorine Niedecker exhibit

Like a cassock-clad
candle-carrying
acolyte
during Lent
I process station
to station
pondering poetry
as forged as nails.

The White Bicycle

It's lurking there in the shadows
of a granary,
ghost of a gone era
when the first farm motors
arrived on tractors
and young girls still rode to town
on two wheels
to fetch supplies home in baskets.

Its basket long gone,
its handlebars like bleached longhorns
on a steer's deserted skull,
it awaits the coolness of night
and its occasional riders,
dead writers.

Tonight it welcomes
its favorite,
the lady in white.

Come quietly after midnight,
watch Emily pedaling
straddling the worn saddle.

You Could Google It

According to a book I'm reading,
The KGB Bar Book of Poems,
in 1997 Boston poet, Ed Barrett
became the second poet ever
to use the word haruspicate
successfully in a poem.

I assume that James McAuley
was the first, since his poem,
Blue Horses, was published in 1946,
contains the word haruspicate,
and seems to be a rather successful poem
if one can judge by the internet searches I've done.

What I don't know is whether any poems
since Barrett's have contained the word
haruspicate, but none show up on a Google search.
Which makes this poem, if successful,
a candidate for third in the line.

(who knows how many unsuccessful ones have been attempted?)

And this poem, successful or not,
is almost certainly the first one
to use the word haruspicate four times.

Dear Internet,

I am not interested in the graduating class 1967.
You've snooped out the fact that I was born in 1949
and assumed that I graduated high school in 1967.
Wrong, I graduated in 1966, skipped a grade;
which may or may not be evidence
that I am smarter than you are.

And I don't intend to demonstrate to you
that I know all 50 states and their capitals.
If you don't know them, look them up yourself.
You're supposed to be so smart.

I also don't care how closely I may be related
to George Washington. He wasn't all he was cracked up to be.
Anyway, not sure I'd be proud of it.

I am somewhat interested in my dad's Uncle Steve,
who allegedly was killed in 1912, when one of the steers
he was driving to market was struck by a train
near Ypsilanti, Michigan, and crushed him
after knocking him from his horse.
One would think that "Killed by Flying Cattle" would be
a banner headline very easy to find,
but you've been no help at all.
Guess I'll have to go to the library. Stupid Internet.

By the way, just because I happen to be shopping
for a new furnace does not mean that I am interested
in buying a Miami Heat basketball jersey,
or a Chicago Fire soccer souvenir.

Finally, although my name is spelled E-D, it does not necessarily follow that I suffer from erectile dysfunction. However, it was helpful to inform me that occasional problems in men over the age of 50 are normal and to be expected. And for that, I thank you.

Caution!

The contents of this poem are hot!
Mishandling may result in serious burns.
To remove this poem from an oven or microwave
the use of a pot holder or oven mitt is recommended.

Open with care. The contents of this poem are under pressure.
Refrigerate after opening.

Due to the risk of injury including possible suffocation,
do not place this poem within reach of infants or children.

Use of this poem is not to exceed 20 minutes.
If experiencing shortness of breath or dizziness,
exit this poem immediately and seek medical attention.

Do not use this poem while under the influence
of drugs or alcohol.

Do not leave this poem unattended in airports.
Refuse to read poems offered to you by strangers in airports.
Report all suspicious poetic activity to the proper authorities.

Wear a seat belt while operating this poem.
The use of airbrakes in the vicinity of this poem is prohibited.
Exceeding the speed limit while reading this poem is illegal
and will result in fines and the loss of points on your poetic license.

Do not attempt to read this poem without first reading
the owner's manual. Doing so will invalidate the stated warranty.

Use this poem only as directed.
Serious or even fatal side-effects may occur.

The most common side-effects include ranting, punning, doggerel, triteness, and obscure references. If experiencing side-effects consult your state's Poet Laureate immediately.

Ask your doctor if your heart is healthy enough to read this poem. Seek immediate medical attention if reading this poem causes an erection lasting more than four hours.

You may cancel your subscription at any time
and receive a full refund. Return the unread portion
to your local library.
Call within the next 10 minutes and receive a bonus poem
at no extra charge. Just pay shipping and handling.

This poem is available daily except for Christmas Eve
and New Year's Eve when you should be reading
Clement Moore and Bobby Burns instead.

Shoes and shirt required.
Enter at your own risk.

You may exit this poem at any time.
Hand stamp is required for re-entry.
The poet accepts no responsibility for injuries
resulting from reading this poem.

For external use only.

This poem was written by a poet
who consumes peanuts and undercooked eggs.

Upon completion,
lather, rinse, repeat.

Spineless Thief

The dictionary you deliver
weighs exactly one pound
bound in hard gray plastic,
pageless.

I request War and Peace and get
the same gray shell,
the same one-pound weight.

The Grapes of Wrath,
The Encyclopedia of Baseball,
The Selected Odes of Pablo Neruda,
I'm finding each without
variation in binding
weight or size.

You invite me to pick up
all five volumes at the same time
and amazingly, together
they remain unchanged,
still pageless.

I hate you!
You spineless thief
of the tactile pleasures of my reading.
You hard-shelled, shelfless library.

Will I need to use
my real books for kindling
in your cold world?

Actually

I don't like the word.

Actually,
I hate how it
has crept into all our conversations:

actually, he's in a meeting

actually, I meant to call you

she actually said that?

Actually?
As opposed to what?

Actually, the word has lost all
its corrective capabilities.

Actually, I can no longer distinguish
it from other fillers:

er…um…ah…well…ya know…actually,
I don't love you anymore.

Poetic Language

I doubt that I will ever see
a fragile word like filigree
ever look so much at home
as it does tucked in a poem.

Another word that feels just right
in a poem, say, about fading light,
if my vocabulary's feeling muscular
the sky, I'd write, looks quite crepuscular.

And when some verse you'd like to rhyme
describing subtle changes over time
should one line end with west or best
close the next with palimpsest.

Next time you see one of these three,
palimpsest, crepuscular, or filigree,
the odds are nine times out of ten
a poem will be the where and when.

Accidental Poem

I discovered it
lying on a sidewalk.
No, discovered isn't right,
I stumbled upon it,
slipped on it,
a banana peel of a poem
just sitting there.

It had been there for days
all slimed up and slippery.
A homeless man with an MFA
in creative writing from Iowa
saw it last week,
recognized it for what it was
but had neither pen nor pencil
so he memorized it.
You can hear him mumbling
some lines to the stray dogs
late at night, behind the soup kitchen.

Others paid it no attention
or avoided it all together,
stepping over it if they did see it.

But me, accidental poet,
I stepped right on it,
slipped on its sliminess
into an embarrassing pratfall,
that left everyone laughing
but me.

The Trouble with America

My bottle of barbecue sauce has two labels.
One reads *Hunts Original,* the other
New Improved Recipe. So, which is it?
Original or Improved? Did they just type
the recipe on a new index card and call it improved?

In the window of Whole Foods
is a banner reading, *All Beer 25% Off*
below that: *Excludes Draft Beer.* All?

Here's the recipe for a drug commercial:
Fifteen seconds of hype followed by
forty-five seconds of disclaimers.
Flu shots may cause nausea and diarrhea.
Anti-depressants could cause suicidal thoughts.
Pneumonia shots might cause fever, chills, nausea
and a weakened immune system.

Eggs were bad for me; now they're good.
In between the bad eggs and the good eggs,
egg yolks were bad, and egg whites were good.
Now it's eat all the eggs you want.
If I live long enough, I may be able to enjoy liver again,
unless the medications I'm taking kill me first.

And now democracy is bad. Wait, let me rephrase that,
this democracy is bad. Wait, let me rephrase that,
this is not democracy. I'm pretty sure it's something else.
We're told it's democracy, but there's so much misleading
information floating around out there.

Thank goodness for the multiple benefits of red wine.
Please, don't tell me anything bad about red wine.

Nosferatu's Garden

If Nosferatu were a gardener
he would raise beets
and beets alone,
fang-rooted Rumanian blood bulbs,
vampire of vegetables.

Sucking redness from radish veins
leaving its innards colorless.
Rutabagas, potatoes, parsnips
are no match for its red-robbing wiles.

Only the longer rooted carrot
has managed through the centuries
to cleave to a bit of orangeness.

There is an eastern European wives' tale
claiming that before the beet bit
you *could* get blood from a turnip.

Bubbling in a borscht bowl,
the beet could sustain our fabled count
through those long cold damselless nights.

Fairy Tale Tabloid

The headline in the Fairyland Gazette screamed:
Bashful Dwarf Reveals All!
The sub-heading: *Shocking hot facts that will scorch
the thatched roof off their quaint cabin!*

Although shy and reserved, it seems he was very observant,
this Bashful, and documented all the goings on
of his diminutive mining mates and their presumably chaste
    hostess.

Tiring of their shenanigans and wanting to strike out on his own,
maybe do a little prospecting solo, in the Sierra Madre perhaps,
and in need of a stake he sold his story to the aforementioned
    gazette.

And since I know you are a fairy tale fan and want the true story,
but would never dream of picking up one of those tabloid rags
no matter how long the checkout line is,
here are the pertinent details of his tale:

The reason that Sneezy kept at it and could get no relief
from his hay fever and allergies with some antihistamines;

the reason that Grumpy's cantankerous demeanor, his depression,
couldn't be relieved with a little Prozac;

and the reason that Sleepy's narcoleptic episodes
were never eased with a dose of Alertec or some
methamphetamines;

the reason for their prolonged suffering was that every time
the medical supply wagon made a delivery and Doc
restocked his cabinet, Dopey raided the place to feed

his ugly little drug habit, which explains his vacant eyes
and the blank stare, but not his silence.

No, what silenced the little one's voice,
according to our timid tattletale,
what shocked the vocals right out of that boy's chords forever,
was the day, in a stupor, he stumbled
into Snow White's room and discovered not only
that her chaste reputation was totally undeserved,
but also what was putting that persistent little smile
on Happy's face.

Licorice Lollipops

April in the upper Midwest
is not a completely cruel month.

The red-winged blackbirds return
to marshland and ditch banks
perched on fencepost
or the tops of winter-dried reeds
guarding ground nests
like Westminster guards standing sentry,
looking all together
like an even skinnier version
of Stan Laurel topped with one of those
big black bearskin hats.

Sometimes what I see is a marsh
sprinkled with long-stemmed
licorice lollipops,
a museum of Giacometti thin men
sporting jet black fedoras,
a cartoonist's easel of anorexic Olive Oyls,
their ebony bouffant dos
with little yellow-piped scarlet barrettes
to hold the flapping cowlicks in place.

Helium

Your parents were a couple of hot heads
blew up at the drop of a match
that nasty Hindenberg incident
the most famous of the many times
they lost control.

But they found their matchmaker
in the sun god, your namesake.

When hydrogen atoms get close
and start feeling good about each other
things heat up in a hurry.

The hotter it gets, the closer they get.
They fuck, they fuse,
and are destroyed by their own passion.
Passing on all of their parts and none
of their traits, they become something
completely different: you.

You lead a long lineage of nobility,
a calm inertia is your greatest asset.

You are uplifting, rising
to every occasion,
great fun at parties.

People lift their voices
and speak very highly
of you.

Eskimo Medicine

My friend Rick is into intuitive
healing. I'm not into it I've
placed all my faith in hard science.

I put intuitive healing
in the same category with colored
auras, copper bracelets, and
(this one I could be mistaken about, I suppose)
acupuncture. Any needles puncturing me
had better be delivering real medicine.

Still, in this harsh winter
when Rick starts preaching
the benefits of intuitive healing
my often frozen ears
sometimes mistakenly hear
Inuitive healing
and that I could see myself getting into.

Inuit healing:
a hot stove
in the middle of an ice house
you and me
naked under sealskin blankets
rubbing noses in the dark.

The Attack of the Pneumonia Gang

A medical western

My doctor told me I needn't worry
about a reaction to the inoculation,
"This is a dead virus vaccine",
she said, as she slipped the needle
into my upper arm.

I thought:
Aside from possibly being
an excellent name for a band,
what good are dead viruses?

Then I figured it this way:
A gang of pneumonia viruses
bent on mayhem and bodily harm
comes riding hard into your territory.
They see a bunch of their buddies
dead, strewn about the landscape,
have a change of heart and turn tail.

Or maybe your internal sheriff
and his deputized posse of immunity enforcers
take this bolus of dead viruses
and string them up from gallows
posted around your epidermal extremities.
They dangle there as a warning to malicious intruders.

And as the sun sinks in the west
and the posse moseys into the Serum Saloon
for a much needed booster shot
the movie credits start to roll.

Under music you see,
Theme Song: *We Were Dead Before She Shot Him,*
recorded and performed by The Dead Viruses.

Handball Elder

In the dry heat of the sauna,
the sacristy of my sport,
like a priest before the mass
I anoint myself.

I dip two fingers into the IcyHot
and bless my right knee
then the left.
Another dip, and I apply
the sacred ointment to my left shoulder.

This regular ritual is followed
by a light blessing
of whatever other body parts
are crying for forgiveness.

Next the vestments.
After shirt and shorts:
two knee braces
an elbow brace
athletic tape
gloves
a headband and eye guards.

I pick up the handball
and process toward the sanctuary
of the court.

After the sacrifice of the game
has been offered
I sit in meditation and pray
for an acolyte

to assist me to the rectory
of the locker room
and the holy waters
of the shower.

Organ Grinder

One donor can save up to eight lives.
—Donate Life Website

But who except an organ grinder
would want these?

Sixty-seven-year-old eyes
cataracted, full of floaters,
astigmatized.

Who would want a graft
of this old skin
easily bruised
paper-thin?

Dry, pocked joints
without cushion
that grind and pop
ache and bind.

Ears ringing with bells
that aren't there.

Brittle brain.

Heart long past its warranty.

Here's the Deal

Don't fold
never fold
call all bluffs
check if you have to
raise when you can
take a hit once in a while.

Renege
(if you think you can get away with it)
stand pat if you must
beg, borrow or mortgage
to stay in the game
but never fold.

Look that hooded bastard
seated across the table
right in his vacant eye sockets
and stare.

Hide your cards
breathe easy
smile slightly
and never
ever
fold.

You'll not be dealt another hand.

Save This Poem

Save this poem
from the darkness.
Put it where
someone might find it,
so that it might live
and not be lost
when we are gone.

Fold it in a book
to be found like
a pressed flower
among your favorite things
many years from now.

And if it is read
in that distant future,
who could then say
the dead do not speak,
the way Ella sings to me
as I write this?
Or the way my mother, gone too,
whispers with the daffodils.

Perhaps someone in that future
would imagine
it was written just for them;
the way I imagine now
that some were written
just for me. Imagine,
if you can.

And so to you who reads this now,
who imagines I write only for you,
I say again:
Save this poem
from the darkness.

Sleep

taps me on the shoulder
and says she wants
to take me to bed.

I tell her I'm just
going to finish
this chapter and then
I'll join her and
she'll get what she's after.

Sleep is impatient
keeps poking me
insisting I pay her
some attention.

I think she is jealous
of my books.

Sleep slips a mickey
into my herbal tea
and has her way with me.

I wake at three and realize
she's left me again.

She's thrown my book
on the floor
and hasn't even bothered
to turn out the light.

II. Salting Our Beers

pacific coast surf
the poet writes in green ink
laced with Chile's tears

Somewhen

Time may be an abstraction, but it helps the days go by.
—John Koethe

The last time I was with Lalo
we were sitting in his Santiago, Chile
living room watching a Pavarotti DVD
tears streaming down our faces
and into our beers.

I was thinking how terribly lucky we were
to be alive. I could tell by his tears
he was thinking the same thing.

And I was thinking how terribly certain
it was that eventually we would not be alive.
He was thinking the same thing. Nessun Dorma
sung with such passion will do that to you.

And now Lalo is dying, but then,
so am I, and just as certainly. Yet no one
would write the sentence: *Ed is dying.*

But who could say I'm dying any slower
than he? Who could say with certainty
that I will outlive him even though
his doctors have stopped treating him
and sent him home to die?

Some philosopher-physicists say that
all things just are. That time is an illusion
caused by our conscious sequential awareness
of what are discreet moments of being.
Everything just is.

Maybe Lalo and I are sitting on that couch
salting our beers somewhen right now.

What does now even mean if time is an illusion?
We're born, we're living, we're dead.
We're laughing, crying, singing, drinking. All now.

Five years, or fifty
or five-hundred.
And what if it were five-hundred?
It's still just one big lucky chance
to live, to love, to be, and then not be.

Let's Train Poets Here

Look around. There is only one thing of danger to you here—poetry.
　　　　　　　　　　　—Pablo Neruda, to Pinochet's soldiers

Isla Negra, Chile, 2009

Let's train poets here, not soldiers,
here at Isla Negra, by the sea.

Let's build a new school of the Americas.
Let's write a new curriculum of love and understanding.

We'll sail the poet's boat into international waters
and discover a planet without flags and borders,
a planet he dreamed of.
Essay question: *Why is the land we return to different?*

We'll study a photo of the earth taken from outer space
and contemplate its fragility and smallness.
Essay question: *Imagine you are an alien discovering Earth.
What life do you hope to encounter there?*

We'll study the economics of exploitation,
climb a mountain and rewrite the sermon to read:
the meek shall inherit the earth…and the mineral rights.

We'll make annual field trips to Georgia,
to that other school of the Americas,
join with those who advocate its closure,
read our poems, sing our songs,
dream a world of peace.

And when graduates of that school
are sent again to raid this place,
may they find nothing
but this memorial to Neruda:
a library full of beautiful, dangerous poetry.

Citizen of the World

for Anthony

Welcome, citizen of Chile, chileno nuevo.

Born in the land of Allende,
open your virgin eyes wide to view the land
that inspired Mistral and Neruda,
and be inspired to do great things.

Welcome, American citizen, new American.

Open your ears to listen to the poetry of Whitman
and Ferlinghetti. Hear what America should be, could be.

Born in the land of Pinochet, open your eager mind
to learn the history of your two countries
and how they are connected; learn the bloody history
of the continents united in your blood.

Welcome, citizen of the world, human being.

Born in the New World, into the infancy of the next new world,
open your young heart and feel the love
of your mother and your father.
Look them over closely and see that flags and borders
can be meaningless.

Carry their love inside of you
and with that love, and their mixed blood,
inspire others, like your arrival inspires your family.

Oh, the great things you will see in your lifetime!

Anthony Hands

One reaches up to me
when I say: *Give me your hand*
as we cross a street
or enter a parking lot

and Anthony repeats my words
in his mother's tongue: *Dame la mano.*

Sometimes we reverse the languages.

On the stairs they both wave grandpa away
and grab the handrail—big boy.

At snack time
they pocket peanuts,
hold out raisins to share,
sign for more milk,

and at story time
they relentlessly grab
for my glasses.

While exploring
they offer up acorns, bottle caps
and other found things for identification.

Clenched tightly,
arms rigid,
they are prelude to a scream.

After the visit
their traced ghosts
wave to me
from the refrigerator.

Questions for Mati

To my 4th grandchild at 6 days old

How can you be so small?
Was your brother ever this small?
How can anyone be this small?
But here you are,
feet bouncing on my fingers
and your head nestled
in the el of my elbow.

Was your father ever this small?
I can't remember.
Is this how I came into the world?

Do criminals and mass-killers
come into the world like this?
Held in the arms of someone who loves them?
How does it go wrong for them?
When do things change?

When do politicians first learn how to lie?

And tell me Mati,
when do bankers and corporate CEOs
lose their little hearts
if there is ever a time
when they lie with their head like this
tucked in their grandfather's arm
their tender toes tickling
his fingertips?

Still Life

On February 27, 2010 an earthquake, magnitude 8.8, struck the central coast of Chile.

In the photos,
taken just hours before the earth shook,
you are smiling,
happy to have a Wisconsin visitor,
happy to talk baseball and American politics.
Happy to introduce someone new
to the flavors of pastel de choclo,
that most authentic of Chilean cuisine,
which sits cooling in front of you,
its thick, sweet, corn crust,
like the crust of Chile, still unbroken,
but bubbling beneath its surface.

Later, after the meal
and the malbec, our friend,
your visitor, walks to his hotel,
and you, your wife, and my grandson
board the metro heading for home,
all of you still smiling,
still unaware
of the earth's deeper motion,
unaware of the trembling night ahead.

Unaware that just off the coast,
frantic fish are already heading
for deeper waters.

Experiment in Valdivia

For Olfa

She stops at every mirror,
in the hall, the hotel lobby, on the street
she uses shop windows, straightens
her hair, cleans her sunglasses,
glosses her lips, smooths a collar.
In between, she searches for another mirror.

But I know she's really looking for words,
words that I will understand, searching
for dictionaries that will translate
what I say to her. Our communication
is quiet and strained, or silent.

She seems to constantly jump to the wrong
translation.
Wait, that's not what I meant.
What I meant was I don't say things right,
which bothers her
because I don't hear things right either.

Three months ago, in Miami,
we communicated better,
but that was an experiment
with no anticipated results.
My Spanish, and her English
should have improved since then.

But here, now, nothing, either way,
is heard correctly.
It's like being in a house of mirrors
for the ears.

Good Night Dad

I wish I could write
a song for my father
as sweet as that Horace Silver tune.
And if I could, and if he were still here,
I could tell him that I understand why
the girls got hugged and kissed
and the boys got a handshake,
and that I always understood
why, and that it wasn't until much later
that I even thought it could have been any different.

I could tell him,
but even now,
I probably wouldn't.

March 31

For Loretta (Bruck) Werstein [7/21/1916–3/31/1992]

I usually start listening
for your whisper
on this anniversary,
but it's the earliest
of early Springs and
you've been on my mind
for weeks now.

It's twenty-five years today
and I can still hear your voice
still celebrate the unlikely luck
that was you in my life.

The forsythia burst forth
and the daffodils
didn't just creep in
between the raindrops
but dropped suddenly
into full bloom
bringing with them
as usual, your voice:

Just look at that yellow!

Supply and Demand

To my brother

How could we have known
those many years ago,
we were sitting on treasure
each with hoe in hand
hoe-boes
hoe-bros
straddling bean rows
in the hot sun
uprooting burdock?

I saw it in Whole Foods today.

BURDOCK ROOT: $1.99 per pound.

$1.99 a pound!
For weeds!

Burdock, that dreadful
water-wasting bane
of soybeans and farm boys.

I can't stand it.

I just got used to paying
for thistle seed
to feed the birds.

Habits

I wonder if the Sisters of the Perpetual Rosary
who have declaimed the decades continuously since 1880
think about the words any more.

Do they awake with the memory of it
put on the habit of it
feel the beads on their fingers before rising
the way an amputee feels his lost leg?

In the morning I still look at the wall
where the clock died a year ago
still listen for your voice
calling me to the table.

In Walked So and So

As I fumble through my folder
frantically searching for a substitute poem
I wonder if Charlie Parker ever
made a last minute change to his play list
scratching, say, *Nancy with the Smiling Face*
or *Sweet Lorraine* and substituting perhaps
Ellington's *In My Solitude*
when a lost love happened
into Birdland
just as the gig was about to begin.

Mars, Venus, and the Green Bay Packers

It's game day and I am walking to Whole Foods
past bars filled with noisy fans
gazing at gigantic TV screens,
and as I pass the Bradford Beach Club
the crowd inside erupts in cheers.

I quickly surmise that the good guys have scored
but then, five steps further on, another elated
(related?) roar is emitted from the open door
of Hooligan's Pub directly across the street.

This temporal distortion puzzles me until I theorize
that the Beach Club's screens are cable fed
while the TVs in Hooligan's are receiving
satellite signals through a dish.

This is just a theory
but suddenly I understand
a communication problem I am having:
me, hard wired for direct input, and her,
a concave bowl searching for signals from the stars.

Prosecuting Attorney

But Mary kept all these things in her heart and thought about them often.
—Luke 2:19

The evidence she has is very clear.
I should be way more careful what I say.
Like Mary, she holds all things in her heart.

No take-backs or expiration dates, that's clear.
Once uttered it's recorded just that way.
The evidence she has is very, very clear.

Think hard, be sure, or else don't even start
to speak or surely later you will pay,
when your Mary reveals things held in her heart.

Remember what you said in September last year?
I don't, and often can't remember yesterday.
But the evidence she has is always crystal clear.

I've got a bit of hard-earned wisdom to impart:
Whether you've a Jane or Joan, a Chris, Renee
or Mary, know she takes all things you say to heart.

When sentence is pronounced just say, *sorry dear.*
A silent bow, is better than constant replay
of what like Mary, is held deep within her heart,
the evidence each time being very, very clear.

Perspectives

He said,
Why don't we turn that
painting of yours one-hundred and
eighty degrees and hang it that
way to see how it looks?

She said,
Are you kidding? That would
be like me asking you to read
one of your poems starting with
the last stanza and going up.

He said,
Why don't we turn that
painting of yours one-hundred and
eighty degrees and hang it that
way to see how it looks?

Revision

How do you know when it's finished,
or at least finished with you?

How do you know,
when each time you see it
you cross out words,
change them,
sometimes changing them
back to what they were before,
and next time back again.
The same two words
                leap-frogging
      leaping over
                leap-frogging
each other
there on the page.

And because you're probably not ever
going to be finished with it,
how do you know
when it's finished with you,

the way she was finished with you,
while you went on,
each time you saw her,
hoping for different words
to come leaping from her mouth.

The Moon is Always Female

—Marge Piercy

Why does the sun get the starry male lead
in the cosmic soap opera
while the moon either
hides her face in his light
or reflects that light
in his absence?

And why is she the temperamental
sensitive one
causing tides of watery emotion,
only very rarely
eclipsing the shining star?

And even then, we mustn't look.
We must avert our eyes
from her boldness.

Certainties

Death and taxes?
I'm not convinced.

Our impending death is just a conclusion
we've come to based on the evidence,
which I will admit is quite compelling,
but, nonetheless, not a logical certainty.

And taxes?
Don't even start.
Their rumored inevitability is merely
governmental propaganda.

No, the only thing we know
for certain, is uncertainty.

Heisenberg's uncertainty principle
got Schrödinger to thinking
about cats in boxes
which led Feynman
to fire subatomic matter
through small slits, asking,
is it a wave or is it a particle?

We don't know until we look,
and it's whichever one we're looking for.

Yes, it's all there in black and white,
proven that we are only certain
of uncertainty.

So what are the chances
of you and me becoming us?

Do you happen to have a boxed cat
we could consult?

Grand Unified Theory

Isn't it strange that light
can also be heavy,
can exhibit properties
of gravity,
attracting things
like a black hole?

I'm caught by the gravity
of your light,
circling. Circling,
like a planet
tethered to a sun,
seeking the light,
the photosynthesis
you cause in me.

Isn't it strange that what attracts
can also repel?
I'm circling, yet held at this distance.
How? By my own motion around you?
By opposing magnetic fields?
By fear of falling into fire?

That I perceive you rising
each day to warm me,
is an illusion,
caused by my ignorance
of the forces at work.

"I'm not where I belong"

For Beth

Well, what can you expect really?

The universe is so vast
and we are so small,
so accidental.

What are the odds
of occupying the proper space
at the correct time?

If we ever get it right,
once in a great while perhaps,
it's like a gift,
a present
of the present.

Sometimes maybe it's terpsing a tango
in Buenos Aires,
and sometimes just talking
with a friend in a tea shop,
but for then, you know
you are where you belong
and it's a gift for sure.

The Geography of Penelope Cruz

I've always wanted to write an ode with this title,
explore the map of her,
plumb the depths of her oceans,
wax poetic about cruising around her globes.

But now, prompted to write it, I think
it might be a bit too risky,
what with Congress the way it is,
and my reputation as a modern, sensitive man
somewhat better than deserved.

Suffice it to say that were she Penelope
to my Ulysses, she'd not grow old
scanning the horizon, waiting for my ship to return.

All my exploits would be home grown.
Each night, a night in port.

Kooser's Groupies

As a teenager my impulse toward poetry had a lot to do with girls.
—Ted Kooser

At the breakfast reading
they call out to hear their favorites
the way girls in the forties begged
Frankie to fly them to the moon,
or in the sixties screamed
for John and Paul to hold their hands.

And a few of them may have ridden
to the moon on Air Sinatra
a time or two,
behind closed bedroom door
phonograph spinning with their dreams.

Many no doubt had dreamed
of George's slender hands
fingering more than
the neck of his weeping guitar.

But a different man sets them
swooning now, a quiet unassuming man
rooted in their heartland.
A man of well-chosen words
that do his singing for him.

And the women call out:
Read, *The Beaded Purse!*
A Jar of Buttons, Mother.
How about *Pearl!?*

Oh, you've got them, Ted.
They may not be girls any longer,
but you've got them.

Venus of Delta

In the hubbub
of the airport screening area,
that kerufflian confusion posing as security,
right in front of me, she bent
to remove her shoes.

It was the bending that did it,
the flesh inside stretching
tightening the denim even more.

Her pose, a picture destined for the dictionary
illustrating callipygian.
This woman's calli
was as pygian as they come.

The goddess Callipygia herself, in the flesh.

I was flummoxed and flamboozled.
Flustered, I left liquids unbagged,
dropped change all over the floor,
frazzled the folks waiting behind me.

After stumbling twice
through the metal detector,
forgetting to remove my belt,
and now completely disassembled,
I was relieved at last
to see exactly what I needed:

Recombobulation Area.

The Picture of Dorian Redwood

Forestry researchers have discovered that redwood trees
produce denser, harder wood, and more of it, as they grow,
to the age of about 1500 years.

—National Geographic

I want to grow old
like a redwood tree
producing harder wood
each day
and more of it.

I want to live
to the age of 1500
rooted and rooting
in Northern California.

I want my biography
to be titled
The Picture of Dorian Redwood.

The story opens
with the discovery
of a portrait
—a painting of
a wrinkled weeping willow
hidden high in my canopy,
and after several centuries
of satisfying sexual adventures,
ends with me being felled
by a jealous logger
suffering from
erectile dysfunction.

Folding Contour Sheets

Look for the corner seams
match them up in pairs
spread your arms wide
and the frustration begins.

Something is not right, a sock
or a pair of underwear
is in one of the pockets
that the corners make.

Shake, and it falls on the floor
but that's not the whole problem.
You've got the corners crossed
and as you try to rearrange things
without losing your grip,
it falls apart—and you start again.

Even the best you've ever done
is not very good; it's bumpy,
bunched up.
Like a puzzle with a few pieces
out of place, it's not solved.

But it's not like your puzzle
with the bent spike and the ring
that you can just put back on the desk
unsolved.

This is more like the friend you can't quite figure out,
The friend you grab by the corners every once in awhile
and gently shake in the hopes you can fold her
into the friend you need.

What you need is resignation.

Just roll the sheet up tight
place it in the linen closet
place the neatly folded flat sheet
and pillow cases on top of it
press down firmly and close the door.

When you get them out again
unroll the contour and pull
it tight to the matress,
the struggle to tame it, forgotten.
That night when you crawl in between
the flat and the fitted, everything fresh and clean:
the sheets, and you, and her,
grab the friend you've never tried to shake or fold,
the friend who seemed to come pre-fitted to you,
the friend who never needed to be solved
and who never needed to solve you.

You're like the spike and ring, forever joined
between perfect clean sheets.

Her Tea Bag Waits

There on the counter
next to the stove
she has placed her tea bag
still worth one strong cup
sitting on a small saucer
next to her now clean mug
which is next to her plate
and butter knife
which are next to the butter
now perfectly softened
which is next to what's left
of our loaf of sour dough bread
which is next to the toaster
which is her way
on her work days
of sharing breakfast with me
the laziest retiree in the world.

Nick Chopper Lays Down His Axe

The Tin Woodman, originally a human, Nick Chopper (the name first appeared in *The Marvelous Land of Oz*, by L. Frank Baum), made his living chopping down trees in the forests of Oz.

For Sylvia

I never saw the woods like this before
every tree sacred, the forest a cathedral.

Yesterday I spied her, a sprite,
a spirited sylph dancing in a clearing
around the altar of a felled trunk.

I was blinded, like Paul on the Damascus Road
forever altered, forever her disciple.

And when my vision cleared
I gazed into the polished metal
of my axe and saw myself
real and true for the first time
a hollow man, heartless
as a money changer
in this wooded temple.

I am the Tin Man
whose tears of remorse
now rust my hinged joints.

I stand here motionless
empty
praying for holy oil
from the sylvan goddess
to liberate my dance of joy.

III. Taking the Needle

Apolitically
the sun and moon rise and set
despite elections

We All Lay Down

On September 21, 2011, Troy Davis was executed by the State of Georgia

I'm not saying Troy Davis is innocent.
Troy Davis said it.
Some witnesses said he was guilty, then recanted.
Said they were coerced by police.
I'm not saying Troy Davis is innocent.
I'm saying there's doubt.

I'm saying murder is murder,
especially state-sanctioned killing.
I'm saying lynching is still legal in Georgia;
ropes, no longer around necks,
strap men to gurneys, hold them there for four hours
while learned judges deliberate.
No mercy.

I'm not saying Troy Davis is innocent.
I'm saying you could have been Troy Davis.
Or me.
Given other circumstances,
Clarence Thomas or Barack Obama
could have been Troy Davis.

I'm not saying Troy Davis is innocent.
I'm saying the state of Georgia is guilty.
I'm saying America is guilty.
I'm saying we're all guilty.

We all lay down on the gurney
and took the needle.

Fuse

All's quiet on the eastern front
as a thin white cloud
an open parenthesis
curves up from the line
separating the gray-blue sky
from the blue-gray lake.

Gradually it begins to glow
red-orange
like a lit fuse.

Slowly the sun,
like a programmed cherry bomb
rising light by light
from the bottom of a Times Square billboard,
climbs out of the lake.

As it crowns into view
the horizon explodes,
flashes brilliant north to south, afire
like a distant war zone
only silently, and with hope.

First World Problem

This is the third straight day
without hot water here
at Lakecrest Apartments
on Milwaukee's east side.
You'd think we were being tortured.

This is not Gitmo
or Stalag Prospect Avenue.
True, there is no hot water
but at least it is not
the drip…drip…drip
of a boarding ordeal.

A secret has been ripped
from our lips:
We are soft-skinned whiners
many generations removed it would seem
from the calloused genes
of our parents and grandparents.

This is not a bombed-out, burned-out
flat in Baghdad and we're in little danger
of being scalded toting
hot water from kitchen stove
to bathroom sink.

Apostrophe S

You slimy serpent-shaped sneak
you sibilant snake in
the dictionary
always starting
something
twice ending
happiness
always wanting
more
plundering pluralizing possessor
you greedy symbol
of the American Dollar
your apostrophe attaching you
to whatever you would possess.

Gardening in Babylon

We dig holes
in human beings
with bullets
and holes in their homelands
with bombs.

And in those holes
we plant seeds
of hatred and revenge.

Yet we are always amazed
when we reap the harvest,
our own sown terror
come to fruition.

Liberation

We are liberating you.
We know you didn't request it, but here we are,
you'll come to love us.

You will be free:
to drink Coke, shop at Wal-Mart
and eat at McDonald's.

Free to assimilate to American culture,
having been freed from the biased,
local control of your own media.

Free to work at a different job
(pardon us, but destroying your old one was a strategic necessity)
employed at one of the military bases we've established
to preserve your new-found freedom.
Or for one of the American companies
contracted to rebuild what our bombs have destroyed.

Eventually, if you earn enough money,
you will be free to travel to America
where you can visit museums, and see
some of your country's national treasures.

They were liberated with you.

When you earn enough money,
and your country has been rebuilt
in the right god's image,
you may want to buy a car.

Then you will be free to drive through
what your country will have become:
the homogenized,
monotonous landscape
that is corporate globalization.

Red-winged Sentry

Cycling through central Wisconsin,
watching mid-May farming;
despite recent rains, fields are being tilled
and planted with corn and soybeans
as streams and ditches drain excess
water from the tiled fields.

Gaining speed on a gentle downslope
I startle a blackbird, standing sentry,
guarding an unseen ground nest.

Like a fighter-jet scrambling to a radar alert,
he is off his fencepost and flying
five feet above and slightly behind me,
red-orange decal in bright yellow piping
glistening in the sunlight.
Chattering away, he escorts me to the end of the fencerow,
the boundary of his responsibility.

I tried my best to explain things to him.

Told him it was an inadvertent encroachment,
not a pre-emptive strike.
That I had no intentions of
leaving behind permanent bases,
stealing his resources
or changing his traditional way of life.

He was having none of my apology.

Droning On

You don't want me to tell you about drones
but I'm going to tell you anyway.

You don't want to think about drones
killing innocent people in Pakistan
drones that you paid for
that we paid for.

Innocent people that thought things would be better
with a different US President
instead they are worse
yes I said worse
especially if you are a dead Pakistani.

And yes, I know you don't want me to tell you about it
that a president you helped elect
that you celebrated and cried over
that our first Black president
is a war criminal
but I'm telling you
and it's true.

You don't want to think about your tax dollars
our tax dollars killing innocent people
innocent by anyone's standard of innocence
as innocent as your grandchild.

You don't want me to tell you
and I don't want to have to tell you
but I don't want to think about it alone.

I want you to tell me
what are we going to do?

Show and Tell

Poetry it is said
should show not tell
but sometimes a little telling
can go a long way.

If I tell you about a man
who beats his wife
abuses his mistress
and fools around in the basement
with his niece, I'd be showing
you a much bigger picture
of the world.

You could tell me about
a starving child you saw
on television
dark skin on bony limbs.
You send money each month
she sends a picture.
Maybe it's her
you're not sure.

Then we could tell each other
about our nephews
who came home from the war
yours without legs
mine with demons
stowed in his backpack.

Fog Forces Cancellation of the Air Show

Milwaukee Journal-Sentinel headline

If only it were that easy
to stop a real bombing raid
mothers all over the world
would pray for bad weather
everyday
to spare their homes
their homelands
their children.

But here on Milwaukee's lakefront
the spectacle is rescheduled for tomorrow.

This roaring assault on eardrums
and sensibilities is nothing
compared to the price paid by others
for the live-ammo show
rain or shine.

Here, parents bring the kids
wave flags
eat ice cream.

Campaign Promises

When I rule the world
which is to say when we rule the world
all of us together
there will be less to pray for
and churches will be converted
to museums and art galleries
with choir loft apartments overlooking
neo-naves of public discourse
pews rearranged to facilitate conversation.

When I rule the world
which is to say when we rule the world
all of us minus those greedy few that rule us now
battleships will be redeployed
some re-flagged as cruise ships
their guns and armor reformed to recreational uses.
Others will be anchored in harbors
and each become a beachfront neighborhood
with promenades lined with flower pots
and libraries where the admirals
once slept their battled dreams.

When we rule the world
all of us together
children will grow up healthy
because doctors will work uninfected
by corporate interests
and the games and laughter of children
will reveal their strong bodies and straight teeth.
Children will all grow up loved
and they will all grow up
and none of them will grow up
to be soldiers.

Fences

There used to be more sides in the world.
Grandpa's barn had four good sides
before it went down in a storm in '87.
Grandpa, too, had sides, a good one and a bad one.
They both went down in '63.

When Uncle Jim took a steer to market,
there were two sides of beef,
a side in his freezer, a side in ours.

There used to be shorter fences in back yards
and neighbors on each side talking to each other.
And if they ever mentioned sides,
it wasn't to say, "you're on the wrong side."

There was your side and my side, but we talked.

And politics? Jesus,
there were all kinds of sides
and lots of middle ground
in the town square.

Now sides are taken, not shared.

Newsmen boast about reporting both sides of the story,
as if there were always only two.

There used to be a sunny side of the street,
a few dead ends, but every street with a sunny side,
not just Park Avenue.

Can you remember?
Can you even imagine it now?
Every street with a sunny side
and all you had to do was cross over.

Playing Cards

In this game the Joker is wild
and diamonds are Trump!
He holds no heart,
uses clubs to beat us,
then hands us a spade,
right before the execution.

Love Trumps Hate

I.
That's what we believe anyway.
Love your neighbor
your enemy even
turn the other cheek
all that jazz.

Our hearts will trump their clubs.
Really?
It's looking pretty bleak lately
but we're holding out hope
because we know
love trumps hate!

II.
We are the winners!
And we just love Trump's hate!
It frees us to be ourselves.
No more hiding
although we kinda like the white hoods.

We love having our free speech back.
We can call a spade a spade
and a Muslim a terrorist.
Clubs suit us.
Oh yes, we're in charge!
And we love Trump's hate!

Another Useless Headline Poem

US Senate Response to Orlando: Nothing.
—The Guardian, June 21, 2016

I've been thinking about flesh
and blood
and guts
and guns
and bullets
and assaults
on our sanity.

And I've been thinking about guts
and guns
and gold
and gilt
and guilt
and gullibility
and gushing blood
and the gumption
it might take
to change things.

And I've been thinking about how
we must not be
disgruntled enough
disgusted enough
about how we must not be
dis-gutted enough
to stop watching the news reports
to stop posting on Facebook
to stop writing ineffective
and useless poems
about it

to finally rise up
and do something real
to change it.

Mine

I say, it's mine. You know who I am.
Mine is mine, and those things you thought were yours?
They're mine.

The mines are mine.
All the mines that miners mined and died in
or out of.
They're mine.
And that mine that is not a mine yet?
That mine you don't want?
It will be a mine, and it will be mine.

Protest and speak out all you want,
I've got my people working on it.
They're mining the constitution.
You didn't think *that* was yours, did you?

I'll sing you part of an old refrain:
This land is MY land,
I forget the rest.

The oil is mine,
the water, mine, even the wind.
I'll meter it and sell it to you,
as soon as you buy all my oil.

Yes, the earth is mine!
And when I'm gone it's going
to stay in the family—inherited.

And don't give me any of that
the meek will inherit the earth crap.
You wanna get yourself crucified?

realchristiansanonymous

If Jesus had a smart phone
would he have been addicted to games
like Angry Peace Doves
instead of hiding in the temple
questioning rabbinical inconsistencies?

Would he never have been lost in the temple
because of the GPS locator on Mary and Joseph's phone?

If Jesus had a smart phone
would he have live tweeted
the sermon on the mount
#lovethyneighbor #inherittheearth

Would he have googled
groceries, Galilee, delivery
and ordered loaves and fishes
brought to the back side of the mountain
and schlepped up by his disciples
to amaze the crowd gathered in front?

If Jesus had a smart phone and a Facebook account
would he have started a page called
RomansOutof Judea! or *HerodGoHome!?*
and would Judas have lurked there
posting hate comments under an assumed identity
then sold him out for 30 pieces of bitcoin?

Would there have been a live stream link
to The Last Supper, during which he would have said,
whenever two or three of you are logged on
to my Facebook page, there I am among you?
or, *take this and re-post it, for this is my cyber-essence?*

If Jesus had a smart phone and a Facebook page
and a Twitter account, would a flash mob
have shown up at the trial shouting, *Release Jesus!*
drowning out the cries for Barabbas?

Would Rome have fallen
and would all empires since have failed too,
hounded by realchristiansanonymous, a group started long ago
by a Nazarene, with a smart phone?

Memo on a Parable

To: The Shepherd
Re: Your Lost Sheep

Let's consider this from his perspective.

Maybe he had a mind of his own.

Maybe he was tired of conforming,
of every time his eyes wandered
feeling the crook of your staff
round his neck.

Maybe he just wanted to be
alone for awhile,
to not be a part of the fucking
flock any more.

Maybe he was sick and tired
of your mid-night advances.

Maybe he was an artist searching
for a tar pit to dye in,
the original black sheep.

Maybe he didn't want to be found.

Maybe you were just afraid
of what songs he'd sing to your flock
across the hills at night.

The P(r)o(ph)et as Chemist

A poet is a prophet on hydrochloric acid
no (r)evolutionary following and no (pH) factor at all,
a prophet lacking a base.

Is anybody listening?

I need to drink milk, avoid vinegar and tomatoes,
swear off citrus, pick up a piece of chalk
get to a blackboard and write

dust off my hands on my tongue
and speak some basic truth.

Is anybody listening?

When Jesus said,
the poor you will always have with you
it was a challenge not an excuse.
Mark and John left out the next line,
for as long as we allow Caesar to rule us,

and when he said,
render unto Caesar the things that are Caesar's.
Think!

Do the poor have anything that belongs to Caesar?

Lint

USDA Plan to Speed Up Poultry-Processing Lines Could Increase Risk of Bird Abuse

—Washington Post headline

Today, folding clothes I thought,
for the first time about where lint comes from.

Mom didn't have a clothes dryer.
Every Monday with wet rag
she wiped the farm dust and bird shit
from metal wires and let the wind and sun
do their work.

And when weather didn't permit
out came the wooden racks, and the furnace
did double duty drying denim.

But here I stand again, like every week
with a hand full of lint.
How many sweaters, sheets
and socks picked thin in forty years?

Not only Hotpoint and Maytag benefit from dryer sales.

And when someone says something tastes like chicken,
what do they mean when chicken doesn't
taste like chicken anymore?

Convenience has a price:
thin clothes
bland food
traffic jams
water faucets you could light on fire

If you doubt the last one you can Google it.

Teaching Women How to Fly

*On December 14, 2010, more than 30 workers died and 100
were injured when they jumped from upper floor windows to
escape a garment factory fire in Dhaka, Bangladesh.*

Your great-grandparents marched
for safety, "Bread and roses!"
after the fire forced the women to jump
from windows at the Triangle shirt factory
in New York City in 1911.

Your grandparents fought and died
for safety, "Bread and roses!"
at Flint in 1937.
Held the GM factory for weeks
to win their union.

Your parents picketed
time and again
for safety, "Bread and roses!"
to protect their unions
in what has become the Rust Belt.

And now women are flying again
falling from factory windows in Bangladesh
while you wait in lines at Walmart
to buy the shirts they were sewing
on the day before they died,
died to make the owners richer.

Owners whose ancestors owned
shirt factories in New York.
Owners who now are looking
for other women,
in even poorer countries,
to teach them how to fly.

Meditation on My Sandwich

The first thing I give attention to is
some farmer somewhere has planted rye
cultivated it, harvested that rye
transported it to a mill where
it was ground into flour
and transported again to a Breadsmith bakery
right here in Milwaukee
where it was fashioned into this bread.
Which means, of course, that other farmers
have tended the cows and chickens
that produced the butter and eggs
that went into the bread,
a van or truck driver delivered the bread
to the neighborhood store where I shop,
a stocker put it on the shelf
a sales clerk rang it up
and a bagger handed it to me.
So many workers played a role
in my lunch, and that's just the bread.

Next, I consider the tuna, harvested in the Atlantic
without harm to the innocent dolphins
(the tuna's crime being its taste and nutritional value)
It was shipped to a port, trucked to a cannery
where it was fileted and canned,
trucked again to a warehouse and trucked again
to the same neighborhood store where it was handled
by the same stockers, clerks and baggers.

The mayonnaise made by my immigrant daughter-in-law
reminds me of all the homemakers of Latin America
and a time when things were made by hand and not machine.

And speaking of immigrants, the spinach is from California
(this being early Spring in Wisconsin)
immigrant harvesters, packagers,
more truck drivers, all doing their part
for this little lunch I eat while I watch
the first freighter of the season
pull into the port of Milwaukee
containing perhaps part of a meal I'll eat next week.

Farmers, harvesters, truckers, bakers, shippers
fishermen, cannery workers, packagers, stockers
clerks and baggers, all contributors to my sandwich.
I wonder, do they earn enough to raise a family?
Are they covered by health insurance?
What do I owe them?
What do we all owe them?

Lorca for Beginners

The mask will dance among columns of blood and numbers, among
hurricanes of gold and the groans of the unemployed who will howl
in the dead of night for your dark time.
  —Federico Garcia Lorca, *Dance of Death*, New York, 1929

The blood and numbers are tallied
on the same sheet of the ledger,
columns on a page titled,
Cost benefit analysis

Worn now by generals
now by politicians
now by corporate leaders
the mask delights and dances
as the numbers roll in:
so many wars
so many lives ruined
so many deaths
so much profit.

Politicians practice their pirouettes
as they wait their turn
to wear the mask
to take the stage
to praise the generals
and shower the CEOs
in blood now turned to gold.

The darkness is ours
and is filled with our howls.

Someone Else

Your neighbor's son is killed in an auto accident
and you give thanks. No, not for that but that
your kids are safe in school. Someone who needs
psychiatric treatment, but can't get it at the VA
walks into a school and kills teachers and kids alike
and it's not your school, not your town.

A co-worker's spouse dies of cancer
a tornado flattens a town in another state
an earthquake kills hundreds in another country.
There's a flood somewhere, a fire somewhere else
a mudslide, a tsunami, a train derails,
all far away.

Bombs are dropped in a distant land and innocent victims
are killed, collateral damage your taxes paid for.
The sons and daughters of people poorer than you
come home in body bags after "volunteering" for a war
they really had no choice about.

An unarmed Black man is killed in St. Louis
then one in Baltimore,
New York, Milwaukee, Cleveland, St. Louis again.
How long has this been going on?
You've read stories of lynchings, Jim Crow laws.
You know about slavery, but assumed
all these things were history.

A gay man is beaten and left in the middle of Wyoming
to die. Gay people in a night club somewhere
are gunned down while dancing. But your kids aren't gay,
any of them…that you know of. It's someone else's kids

someone else's house
someone else's town
someone else's war
someone else's country
someone else's miserable fortune.

Then one day as you pull your Escalade
into a Big Box parking lot and grab
your wallet or your purse, you pause
before you turn off the radio. An ice shelf
the size of New Jersey has dropped
into the Artic Ocean off Greenland.
Another the size of Florida is about to drop
off Antarctica. They say it's too late
there's no going back now.
And something shifts inside you.

That night you have a dream,
or rather you wake up from a dream
that you always had thought was someone else's nightmare.

We're all doomed and you realize too late
that it's not been someone else at all.
That it's been you all along. That it's been us.
That what wasn't you, what had always seemed to you
to be happening to someone else
was happening to you all along.

Legacy

Who will survive us?

Of the mammals, not many.
Dolphins and whales, probably,
if they can take the heat.
Maybe some of the more verminous rodents.

A few amphibians and reptiles
but they'll need a lot of adaptability
to hostile environments.

Insects? Sure, especially beetles.
There are over 350,000 species
of beetles! Some of them
will surely make it.
And cockroaches, that's a given.

Bacteria. Ah, bacteria!
They don't even *need* oxygen.
Let's toast the lowly anaerobic bacterium.
Now, there's a survivor.

Sage Advice

If aliens ever visit us, I think the outcome would be much as when Christopher Columbus first landed in America, which didn't turn out very well for the Native Americans.
　　　　　　　　　　　　　　　—Stephen Hawking

Better we should remain anonymous,
not broadcast our presence to outer space.
Visitors could turn out to be like us.

We have a history of aggressiveness
when arriving in a stranger's place.
Better to remain anonymous.

We've raped and pillaged, spread contagious
diseases, attacked unfamiliar beliefs and races.
What if they turned out to be like us?

We could be the victims of outrageous
acts, wiped out, enslaved, our planet laid waste.
Mr. Hawking advises: remain anonymous.

Aliens might arrive, acting onerous,
purely evil, lacking grace.
Even worse than just like us.

Shouldn't we protect against potential loss?
Perhaps play it safe in any case?
Much better to remain anonymous
than risk attracting aliens that act like us.

Austerity

The text of this poem has been appropriated as a payment of debts owed.

NOTE:

What if, like other states, the state of poetry were in default?
Poets everywhere would be in debt.
A word lifted here, a phrase there,
a borrowed reference
and pretty soon it would start to add up.

The lenders, wildly rich
with words piled high in library vaults
(words like money, gold, jewelry,
estates, off-shore bank accounts,
portfolios and Porsches),
would lend to us
at ever-increasing interest rates.

We would continue to write,
but eventually our words would
disappear as we wrote them,
repossessed.

We would be left with only titles,
signifying not our ownership
but our mounting debts,
and these few words: austerity,
crisis, foreclosure, unemployment,
hunger, poverty, war.

Words that would never be taken from us.

Your Cue

God is a million monkeys
chain-smoking Camels
flailing at Underwood keyboards
and since God has always existed
he's been flailing away a long time.
So can you really be surprised
that he eventually churned out copy
with some semblance of plot
or that he finally got around
to writing you in as a character?

Now that you are here you can see
that you were inevitable.

The surprise of your existence
is no reason to get gaga
over this pack of primordial primates
because god has absolutely no idea
what he is doing.

If he had any idea, any design,
operated with any logic,
would he have conceived of babies
blown to bits right out of their mothers' arms,
nine and ten-year-old boys
conscripted to die holding rifles,
sixteen-year-old sex slaves?

And when you are written out of the story
and you will be
soon, too soon,
don't go thinking that you'll be
written into some heavenly sequel.

This is it,
your one appearance.
No one else holds your script.
You are the only one that knows your role.
This is your one chance.

Speak!

About the Author

Ed Werstein, spent years in manufacturing and union activity before his muse awoke and dragged herself out of bed. He advocates for peace and against corporate power. He is the East Region VP of the Wisconsin Fellowship of Poets and a member of the Hartford Avenue Poets. Ed's poetry has appeared in *Verse Wisconsin, Blue Collar Review, Stoneboat* and *Gyroscope Review* among others. His chapbook, *Who Are We Then?,* was published in 2013 (Partisan Press).

www.ingramcontent.com/pod-product-compliance
Lightning Source LLC
Chambersburg PA
CBHW071057090426
42737CB00013B/2361